INTERACTION OF COLOR

Josef Albers

Interaction of Color

Text of the original edition

with selected plates

Yale University Press

New Haven and London

Designed by Norman Ives
and set in Baskerville type.
Printed in the United States of America by
The Murray Printing Co., Forge Village, Mass.

Distributed in Great Britain, Europe, and Africa by
Yale University Press, Ltd., London; in Canada by
McGill-Queen's University Press, Montreal; in Latin
America by Kaiman & Polon, Inc., New York City;
in India by UBS Publishers' Distributors Pvt., Ltd., Delhi; in
Japan by John Weatherhill, Inc., Tokyo.

THIS BOOK IS MY THANKS TO MY STUDENTS

Table of contents

Preface

In 1963 when Yale University Press published *Interaction of Color* -- after
we had worked together on it for 8 years -- it had 2 surprising features,
a physical one, namely its weight of 22 English pounds, and an
economic one, its price of $200. Both were caused by the large number
of color plates and both immediately suggested a pocket edition
which would be more convenient in regard to both features.

I first planned for a German translation of the main text of the book
(which comprised only 80 pages), which I repeatedly revised myself.

Although the original edition was sold out after 5 years (despite a
final increase of price), 2 years later, in mid-September of 1970, the
publishing house of DuMont Schauberg of Cologne, West Germany,
announced, at the Frankfurt International Book Fair, publication of an
illustrated paperbound German edition of the main text of *Interaction
of Color*. Immediately thereafter Yale University Press decided to
publish a similar English paperback.

It is understood that an inexpensive edition of the main text permits only
a small number of the 150 large color studies included in the original edition.

Now, since the English paperback will contain, for practical reasons, the
same 10 color plates (including the 2 cover illustrations) of the German
version, I have been asked to explain the purpose of these color studies
and relate them to the text.

Although I was not consulted about the selection of those 10 plates, I was
very pleased to find on the front cover a most typical Interaction study.
Typical, because it demonstrates that the author of the original study
(a student in my color course at Yale University) understood his task well
and solved it convincingly (Plate XVII-1).

What you see on the cover is a colorful square subdivided horizontally
and vertically into 4 similar squares -- 2 different reds (placed diagonally)
and a deep green and a pale yellow. At the center these 4 colors appear
to be overlapped by another square (also vertically placed) of a transparent
material (perhaps cellophane or acetate) which casts slight shadings
on the 4 colors underneath.

On the right of this transparent square, a longish triangle is folded
toward the center so that a doubled transparence occurs which causes a
doubled shading on the underlying red and yellow.

What the observer does not realize in looking at these single and doubled
shadings is that there is no transparent material whatsoever, because all the
color papers used in this study are absolutely opaque, that is, non-transparent.

Thus, there are not just 4 colors plus a colorless transparent material,
but there are 6 additional precisely related opaque shades: 2 at the left,
green and red, and at the right 2 for the other red and 2 more shades
for the yellow. With this, the author of this study proves to himself that
he is able to make us see what he wants us to see -- less (no transparence)
or more (6 opaque shades).

I have explained this cover study, consisting of 10 appropriately related
color papers, in such detail in order to prove at the beginning that -- with
color -- "we do not see what we see." Because color, as the most relative
medium in art, has innumerable faces or appearances.

To study them in their respective interactions, in their interdependence,
will enrich our "seeing," our world -- and ourselves.

Of the 9 remaining color reproductions within the book and on the back
cover, I would like to comment first on the two numbered IV-3, because they
present one of the most fundamental and therefore one of the first
exercises in my color course.

For an easier comparing of their respective colors (namely, in horizontal
direction), turn the book so that the left page with the 2 green grids appears
above the study with the 2 small dark rectangles in the center.

The problem to be solved here is to "see" one and the same color on 2 grounds of 2 different colors in such a way that the lower ones (in deliberately small amounts on large grounds) become unlike each other and therefore look different, and, if possible, "incredibly" different.

To most observers the apparent difference in color of the grids in the upper study is more obvious. In order to make the change within the lower pair more noticeable, do not compare their centers by moving your eyes back and forth. Instead, try to see the centers simultaneously by staring at a midpoint of the boundary between the blue and yellow grounds. In this manner you can also see the upper study more clearly.

If someone claims that he can see that the 2 central colors are the same either by shifting his eyes or by staring at the midpoint, he is fooling only himself.

If you wish to see the central colors isolated from their background, close the fingers of both hands to make tubes with small peepholes at the far ends, then place the small holes close to the central colors. You can again see that they are alike despite looking at them by moving your hands and eyes back and forth.

To mention here some exercises which follow: After making 1 color appear to be 2 colors, we try to make 3 colors look 2, or 3 colors like 4, and -- most exciting -- 2 different colors are made to look alike.

All these and similar color deceptions result from 1 phenomenon, the "after-image." To experience it very clearly, let us observe the double-page reproduction VIII-2.

First, in order to prepare for the second part of this demonstration, cut out in red and white color paper 2 equal circles (of ca. 3-inch diameter) and mark their centers with a small black dot.

Then paste them -- horizontally related -- the red circle to the left and the white one to the right, on the blackboard or a piece of black paper or black cardboard, ca. 10 inches high and 20 inches long, with about equal amounts of black before, between, and after the two circles.

Now, by staring steadily at the marked center of the red circle (up to half a minute) one soon discovers how difficult it is to keep the eye fixed on a point. After a while, moon-sickle shapes appear, moving along the circle's periphery. In spite of this, one must continue to focus on the red center point in order to assure the desired experience.

Suddenly, one shifts the focus to the center of the white circle. Then from the class one usually hears noises which indicate surprise or astonishment. This happens because all normal eyes suddenly see green or blue-green instead of white. This green is the complementary color of red or red-orange.

The phenomenon of seeing green (in this case) instead of white is called after-image, or simultaneous contrast.

Second, on the left are yellow circles of equal size which touch each other and which fill out a white square. On the right is an empty white square of the same size. Each is on a black ground.

After staring for half a minute at the left square, one shifts the focus suddenly to the right square. Here one experiences a very different after-image. Instead of seeing the complement of the yellow circles (blue), diamond shapes are seen -- the leftover shapes of the circle -- in yellow. This illusion is a double and thus reversed after-image, sometimes called contrast reversal.

A superficial look at plate XI-3 may indicate that it has to do again with color mixture and with color transparence, as demonstrated in the discussion of the front cover. Physically, this study consists of a grid of 3 horizontal stripes of the same yellow, plus 3 vertical stripes of 3 other colors -- green, violet, and red. All stripes are of equal size and shape and are equidistant.

Optically, these stripes cross each other in 9 equal squares which are mixtures of the crossing colors and which lead us consequently to distinct spatial readings. A close observation of the 3 upper mixture squares, and particularly their edges, will show that their *horizontal* boundaries are the hardest or "loudest" ones.

Moving then to the lowest yellow stripe, we notice here that the *vertical* edges are most pronounced.

Such a differentiation makes us read the top yellow stripe in *front* of the vertical stripes, and the bottom yellow *behind* the vertical stripes.

Now, speculating about the placement of the yellow row in the middle, we may squint our eyes and discover that, despite the strong influence of the white paper ground, we are able to read either the yellow in front or the 3 vertical colors in front (or either behind the others). Which leads us to a spatial placing of both on the same level -- in other words, an optical penetration. This theoretically means: We now arrive at the important but rare "middle mixtures."

Although such a study demands an extravagant effort of 13 different paper colors (and all precisely chosen), it provides a thorough training for our eyes, which I hope will lead to similar studies of this problem.

Now, reproduction XV-2 comes in handy because it presents clearly some middle mixtures, namely in the closely related 3 carmine reds placed between the central dark red and the outer light pink.

When you focus on these 3 reds by staring into the pink you will discover that all 3 appear darker toward the outer edge, and also lighter toward the inner edge. You will see that they refer with their outer half to their inner color neighbor -- dark red; and with their inner half to their opposite color neighbor -- pink.

Thus the slightly similar reds demonstrate what we call a color interpenetration. The concave curves cut into the outer 4 reds are an optical encouragement to read their "fluting" effect -- as in the grooves of Doric columns of Greek renown.

Of the 2 remaining reproductions XVIII-1 and XXII-2, I regret that the first one, as a lone "free" study example, cannot prove that our free color trials -- as homework and independent of class exercises -- do not lead to or result in a "class," or "school," or "teacher" style of work, as has been predicted by incompetent judges.

"Free" studies, in which the whole class works with a given set of 3 or 4 color papers (taken from an early study accepted by the class), demonstrate such an incredible variety of independent work as rarely happens in classes whose students are exposed only to so-called self-expression and not subjected to obligatory class exercises, who are therefore without the training that comes from constant comparing from student to student.

As for reproduction XXIII-2, let me mention first that the screen print reproduction of the original study in the complete edition of *Interaction of Color* was a striking proof that precise, equal light-instensity of 2 colors (incorrectly called "equal value") makes invisible the boundary between them. This is a very rare but a most exciting color experience. Unfortunately, its reproduction here in "3-4 color reproduction" serves only as a warning not to apply a photomechanical process to such color delicacies.

In order to end on a more positive note, I invite serious color students to alter the reproduced grey-violet and grey-green of this study toward equal light-intensity so that the small triangles of the underlying design almost dissolve into the ground. It is a most difficult task, but worth trying.

And I am really pleased that the Goethe Color Triangle is shown here on the back cover, and more, that the reproduction permits us to follow its great subdivisions and Goethe's sensitive characterization of the various groups (see page 67).

In order to appreciate the beautiful color subdivisions and the very subtle moods Goethe distinguished in them, cover on the color reproduction the spaces represented by the empty white spaces of the five upper triangles of the diagram.

Notice also that Goethe's arrangement of 9 basic colors is probably the only one demonstrating the relatedness of primary to secondary plus tertiary colors -- in 2 dimensions.

J.A.

Orange, Connecticut
1971

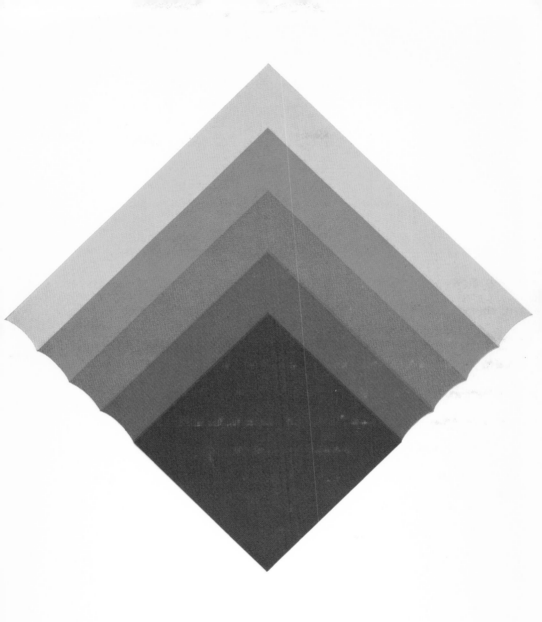

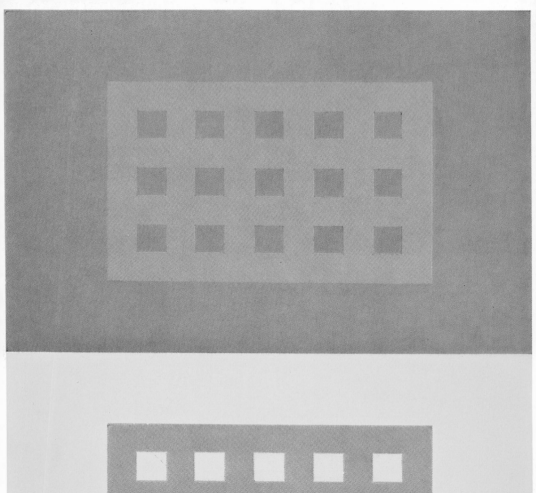

IV - 3

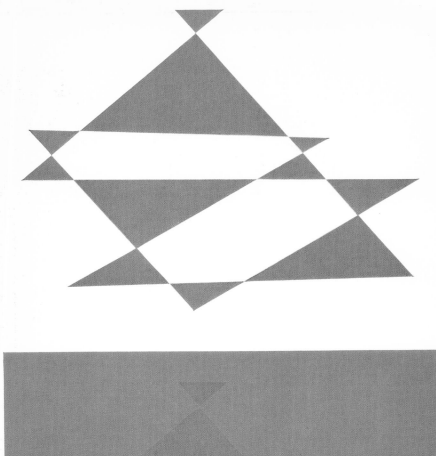

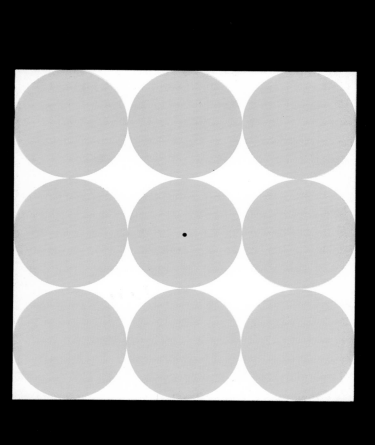

.

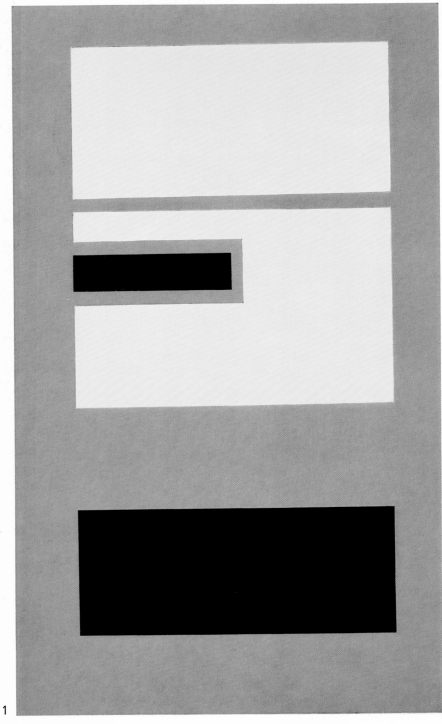

XVIII - 1

Introduction

The book "Interaction of Color" is a record of an experimental way
of studying color and of teaching color.

In visual perception a color is almost never seen as it really is
-- as it physically is.
This fact makes color the most relative medium in art.

In order to use color effectively it is necessary to recognize
that color deceives continually.
To this end, the beginning is not a study of color systems.

First, it should be learned that one and the same color evokes
innumerable readings.
Instead of mechanically applying or merely implying laws and rules
of color harmony, distinct color effects are produced
-- through recognition of the interaction of color --
by making, for instance,
2 very different colors look alike, or nearly alike.

The aim of such study is to develop -- through experience
-- by trial and error -- an eye for color.
This means, specifically, seeing color action
as well as feeling color relatedness.

As a general training it means development of observation and articulation.

This book, therefore, does not follow an academic conception
of "theory and practice."
It reverses this order and places practice before theory,
which, after all, is the conclusion of practice.

Also, the book does not begin with optics and physiology of visual perception,
nor with any presentation of the physics of light and wave length.

Just as the knowledge of acoustics does not make one musical
-- neither on the productive nor on the appreciative side --
so no color system by itself can develop one's sensitivity for color.
This is parallel to the recognition that no theory of composition by itself
leads to the production of music, or of art.

Practical exercises demonstrate through color deception (illusion)
the relativity and instability of color.
And experience teaches that in visual perception there is a discrepancy
between physical fact and psychic effect.

What counts here -- first and last -- is not so-called knowledge
of so-called facts, but vision -- seeing.
Seeing here implies Schauen (as in Weltanschauung) and is coupled
with fantasy, with imagination.

This way of searching will lead from a visual realization
of the interaction between color and color
to an awareness of the interdependence of color with form and placement;
with quantity (which measures amount, respectively extension
and/or number, including recurrence);
with quality (intensity of light and/or hue);
and with pronouncement (by separating or connecting boundaries).

The table of contents shows the order
in which exercises usually lead our investigation.

Each exercise is explained and illustrated --
not to give a specific answer,
but to suggest a way of study.

I Color recollection -- visual memory

If one says "Red" (the name of a color)
and there are 50 people listening,
it can be expected that there will be 50 reds in their minds.
And one can be sure that all these reds will be very different.

Even when a certain color is specified which all listeners have seen
innumerable times -- such as the red of the Coca-Cola signs which is
the same red all over the country -- they will still think of
many different reds.

Even if all the listeners have hundreds of reds in front of them
from which to choose the Coca-Cola red, they will again select
quite different colors. And no one can be sure that he has found
the precise red shade.

And even
if that round red Coca-Cola sign with the white name in the middle
is actually shown so that everyone focuses on the same red,
each will receive the same projection on his retina,
but no one can be sure whether each has the same perception.

When we consider further the associations and reactions
which are experienced in connection with the color and the name,
probably everyone will diverge again in many different directions.

What does this show?

First, it is hard, if not impossible, to remember distinct colors.
This underscores the important fact that the visual memory is very poor
in comparison with our auditory memory. Often the latter is able
to repeat a melody heard only once or twice.

Second, the nomenclature of color is most inadequate.
Though there are innumerable colors -- shades and tones --
in daily vocabulary, there are only about 30 color names.

II Color reading and contexture

The concept that "the simpler the form of a letter the simpler its reading"
was an obsession of beginning constructivism. It became something
like a dogma, and is still followed by "modernistic" typographers.

This notion has proved to be wrong, because in reading we do not read
letters but words, words as a whole, as a "word picture."
This was discovered in psychology, particularly in Gestalt psychology.
Ophthalmology has disclosed that the more the letters are differentiated
from each other, the easier is the reading.

Without going into comparisons and details, it should be realized that words
consisting of only capital letters present the most difficult reading --
because of their equal height, equal volume, and, with most, their equal width.
When comparing serif letters with sans-serif, the latter provide an uneasy reading.
The fashionable preference for sans-serif in text shows neither historical
nor practical competence.

First, sans-serifs were designed as letters not for texts but for captions,
when pictorial reproductions were introduced with stone lithography.
Second, they produce poor "word pictures."

INTERACTION OF COLOR   Interaction of Color

INTERACTION OF COLOR   Interaction of Colo

This illustrates that clear reading depends upon the recognition of context.

In musical compositions,
so long as we hear merely single tones, we do not hear music.
Hearing music depends on the recognition of the in-between of the tones,
of their placing and of their spacing.

In writing, a knowledge of spelling has nothing to do with an understanding
of poetry.

Equally, a factual identification of colors within a given painting
has nothing to do with a sensitive seeing
nor with an understanding of the color action within the painting.

Our study of color differs fundamentally from a study which anatomically
dissects colorants (pigments) and physical qualities (wave length).

Our concern is the interaction of color; that is, seeing
what happens between colors.

We are able to hear a single tone.
But we almost never (that is, without special devices) see a single color
unconnected and unrelated to other colors.
Colors present themselves in continuous flux, constantly related to
changing neighbors and changing conditions.

As a consequence, this proves for the reading of color
what Kandinsky often demanded for the reading of art:
what counts is not the what but the how.

III Why color paper -- instead of pigment and paint

When, more than 20 years ago, this systematic study of color was begun,
it occurred almost as a matter of course that the studies would be done
in color papers. At that time there was some concern among teachers
that students might be reluctant to substitute paper for paint.
Since then, obviously, the attitude of students -- and of teachers --
has changed.

In our studies, color paper is preferred to paint
for several practical reasons. Paper provides innumerable colors
in a large range of shades and tints ready for immediate use.
Though a large collection is needed, it is not expensive to assemble
when one does not rely on large prepared paper sets
representing specific color systems, such as the Munsell or Ostwald Systems
(the least desirable are "tuned" sets, claiming to be failure-proof).

Sources easily accessible for many kinds of color paper are waste strips
found at printers and bookbinders; collections of samples of packing papers,
of wrapping and bag papers, of cover and decoration papers. Also, instead
of full sheets of paper, just cutouts from magazines, from advertisements
and illustrations, from posters, wallpapers, paint samples,
and from catalogues with color reproductions of various materials will do.
Often a collective search for papers and a subsequent exchange of them
among class members will provide a rich but inexpensive color paper "palette."

What are the advantages of working with color paper?
First, color paper avoids unnecessary mixing of paints, which is often difficult,
time-consuming, and tiring. This is true not merely for beginners alone.

Second, by not exposing the student to discouraging failures of mixing
and imperfect matching of spoiled paints and papers, we not only save
time and material, but, more important, gain a continued active interest.

Third, color paper permits a repeated use of precisely the same color without the slightest change in tone, light, or surface quality. It permits repetition without disturbing changes caused by varying application of paint (thinner or thicker -- even or uneven); without traces of hand or tool resulting in varying density and intensity.

Fourth, working with color paper rarely demands more equipment than paste (heavy rubber cement is best), and a single-edged razor blade instead of scissors. This eliminates tools and equipment for handling paints, and therefore is easier, cheaper, and more orderly.

Fifth, color paper also protects us from the undesired and unnecessary addition of so-called texture (such as brush marks and strokes, incalculable changes from wet to dry, or heavy and loose covering, hard and soft boundaries, etc.) which too often only hides poor color conception or application, or, worse, an insensitive color handling.

There is another valuable advantage in working with color papers instead of with paints: in solving our problems again and again we must find just the right color which demonstrates a desired effect. We can choose from a large collection of tones, displayed in front of us, and can thus constantly compare neighboring and contrasting colors. This offers a training which no palette can provide.

IV A color has many faces -- the relativity of color

Imagine in front of us 3 pots containing water, from left to right:

WARM   LUKEWARM   COLD

When the hands are dipped first into the outer containers,
one feels -- experiences -- perceives -- 2 different temperatures:

WARM (at left)   (at right) COLD

> Then dipping both hands
> into the middle container,
> one perceives again
> 2 different temperatures,
> this time, however,
> in reversed order

(at left) COLD -- WARM (at right)

though the water is neither of these temperatures, but of another, namely

LUKEWARM

Herewith one experiences
a discrepancy between physical fact and psychic effect called,
in this case, a haptic illusion -- haptic as related to the sense of
touch -- the haptic sense.

In much the same way as haptic sensations deceive us, so
optical illusions deceive. They lead us to "see" and to "read"
other colors than those with which we are confronted physically.

To begin the study of how color deceives and how to make use of this,
the first exercise is
to make one and the same color look different.

On the blackboard and in our notebooks we write:
        Color is the most relative medium in art.

Challenging examples of very surprising color changes are shown.
Then the class is invited to produce similar effects

but is not given reasons or favorable conditions.
It starts, therefore, on a trial-and-error basis.

Thus, continuing comparison -- observation -- "thinking in situations" --
is promoted, making the class aware that discovery and invention
are the criteria of creativeness.

As a practical study we ask that 2 small rectangles of the same color
and the same size be placed on large grounds of very different color.

Soon, these first trials are collected and separated into groups
of more and less promise.
The class will become aware that change is a result of influence.
The influencing color is distinguished from the influenced color.

It is discovered that certain colors are hard to change, and
that there are others more susceptible to change.

We try to find those colors which are more inclined to exert influence
and to distinguish them from those which will accept influence.

A second class exhibition of more advanced results should clarify
that there are 2 kinds of changing influences working in 2 directions,
light on the one side and hue on the other. And both occur simultaneously --
though in varying strength.

Since 2 pieces of the same paper, therefore of the same color,
are to appear different -- and, if possible, incredibly different --
we must compare them under equal conditions.
The only colors which are factually different are the large grounds,
though they are alike in size and shape.

Because of the laboratory character of these studies
there is no opportunity to decorate, to illustrate, to represent anything,
or to express something -- or one's self.

Here, successful studies present a demonstration. Since they cannot be
misread or misunderstood, they prove understanding both
of the principle involved and of the materials to be manipulated.

(See Plates IV -- 3.)

It should be clear that, with these exercises and all others to follow, whether or not we arrive at a pleasant or harmonious color combination is unimportant.

Precision and clean execution are required for all finished studies. To avoid destroying the desired effect, small pieces of paper on small grounds should not be used.
Arrangements such as the one shown below disguise the desired effect and lead to confusion:

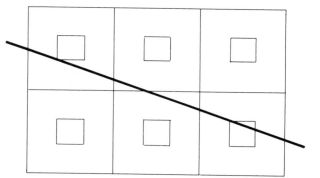

NO

Such studies shown separately in pairs may demonstrate clearly
the desired effects. But interlocked in the tile pattern above,
their illusional effects annul each other because of:

a) The simultaneous influence from too many directions --
    from left and right, and above and below;

b) The unfavorable distribution of area between the influencing
    and the influenced color.

Consequently, such presentation lacks both sight and insight.

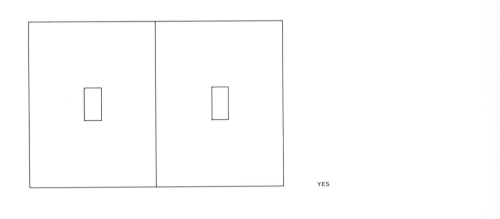

YES

V Lighter and/or darker -- light intensity, lightness

If one is not able to distinguish the difference between a higher tone
and a lower tone, one probably should not make music.

If a parallel conclusion were to be applied to color, almost everyone
would prove incompetent for its proper use. Very few are able to distinguish
higher and lower light intensity (usually called higher and lower value)
between different hues. This is true despite our daily reading of numerous
black-and-white pictures.

Since the discovery of photography and particularly since the development
of photomechanical reproduction processes, we are exposed -- more and more
every day -- to pictures from all over the world, the world seen and unseen,
visible and invisible.

These pictures, which are predominantly "black and white,"
are printed in only 1 black on a white ground. Visually, however,
these pictures consist of grey shades of the finest gradations
between the poles of black and white. These shades penetrate each other
in varying degrees.

With the tremendous increase in pictorial information
-- through newspapers, magazines, books -- we receive a training
in the reading of lighter and darker tones of grey as has never before
existed. With the growing interest in color photography and color reproduction,
a parallel training in the reading of lighter and darker color is on the way.

However, it is still true that only a minority can distinguish
the lighter from the darker within close intervals
when obscured by contrasting hues or by different color intensities.

In order to correct a prejudice common among painters and designers --
that they belong to that minority --
we have the students test themselves. We confront them
with several pairs of color, from which they are to select and to record
which color in a pair is the darker.

The darker one, it is explained, is visually the heavier one, or the one containing more black, or less white. It should be mentioned that the students are encouraged to abstain from making a judgment in any case of doubt. It may also demonstrate that not voting can have a positive meaning.

Though there have always been advanced painting students in the basic color class, the result of this test has remained constant for a number of years: 60% of the answers are wrong and only 40% are right, not counting the undecided cases.

By this experience we are led to the next task: To find colors about which we cannot say immediately which is the lighter or darker. These colors are collected and pasted in pairs, and observed again and again until their light-dark relationship is clearly recognized.

In cases where a decision seems impossible, an after-image effect may be helpful. 2 color sheets are put on top of each other in this way:

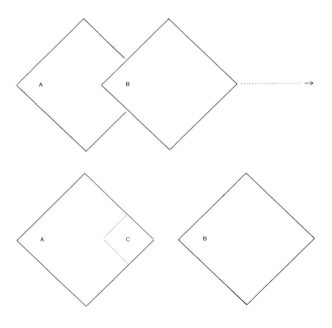

Focus longer than the eye wants to on the covering corner (B) of the
upper paper and then quickly remove this upper sheet. If area (C)
now appears lighter than area (A), then the upper paper is the darker --
and vice versa. After this, repeat the experiment with the papers in
reverse order. Frequently only 1 of the 2 reversed comparisons
reveals the true relationship.

The usual results (60% wrong) are disillusioning as well as revealing.
Voting for the wrong color often needs cover or compensation; also,
the disappointment of wrong answers encourages doubts.
The doubts often are directed, not against one's own judgment, but against
the competence of the teacher: are his answers the right ones?

As the test is to prove whether one has a trained eye or not,
the pairs of color presented for discrimination are not easy to decipher.
Within the pairs there is no equal light intensity
because the conclusive question to be expected from a class is:
are there equal light values within these couples?
The answer is No.

Another unavoidable question is: will a photograph of these colors
reveal their true relationship and thus give the final proof?
The answer again is No.

This answer will remain true for black-and-white
as well as color photographs, because the sensitivity
and consequently the registration of the retina of an eye is different
from the sensitivity and registration of a photographic film.

Normally, black-and-white photography registers all lights lighter
and all darks darker than the more adjustable eye perceives them.
The eye also distinguishes better the so-called middle greys,
which in photography often are flattened if not lost.

As an example we showed our class 2 different reproductions of the
same Ensor painting, "Masks Confronting Death," of 1888. The first
appeared in the catalogue of an Ensor exhibition, the other in a
newspaper report on the same exhibition.

The first, the larger and more official reproduction, in very fine screen
on coated paper, presumably would be considered more representative than
the second, smaller reproduction in a coarser screen and on the
cheapest paper.

But the latter was not only much more correct in its whole tonality;
it also showed clearly 1 more mask, face, or head which the more
expensive, so-called high-key reproduction blotted out entirely -- a small
but complete frontal face, lighter than all the others and separated
from them, near the left picture edge.

This shows what a higher key in light can lose in photography.

The greatest advantage the eye has over photography
is its scotopic seeing in addition to its photopic seeing.
The former means, briefly, the retinal adjustment to lower light conditions.

Color photography deviates still more from eye vision
than black-and-white photography. Blue and red are overemphasized
to such an extent that their brightness is exaggerated.
Though this may flatter public taste, the result is a loss
in finer nuances and in delicate relationships.
Whites rarely appear white but usually look greenish.
This makes color slides of Mondrian paintings unbearable.

For practical reasons, certain groups of our color reproductions in the
original edition are done in 4-color process which presents subdivided,
optically intermixing transparent colors instead of the opaque colors
which are characteristic of most of our studies.

Gradation studies -- new presentations

With the experience that often we are unsure and thus unable
to distinguish between lighter and darker in color, it appears appropriate, even
necessary, to develop a more discriminating sensitivity. To this end,

we study gradation by producing so-called grey steps, grey scales, grey ladders. These demonstrate a gradual stepping up or down between white and black, between lighter and darker.

For such exercises, we first collect as many greys in paper as possible, and preferably independent of commercial grey sets, which usually offer a too limited choice, or, worse, unequal steps. Rich sources for many paper greys are black-and-white reproductions from popular magazines.

Selecting from them smaller and larger areas of as many greys as possible, we will be taught first that photography registers and measures light and dark differently from our eyes. That it turns darks darker and lights lighter means, besides a generalization toward the polar contrasts, a loss of the visually more interesting middle greys. Thus, such reproductions confront us with a dominance of very heavy and very light greys, and a consequent scarcity of middle greys.

These cutouts are to be arranged in gradations as described. The softer the steps appear, and the more equal the steps are, the more valuable and convincing the study. As any lines or empty spaces between the steps interfere with a direct comparison, such separating in-betweens prove nonsensical. We also reject the still-recommended but misleading stepping-up of thin layers of water colors or India ink, as explained in Chapter XX. In order to avoid such mistakes, and also any mechanical repetition of the too-familiar illustrations of color books, we aim at a more creative, more challenging, more instructive presentation. Thus we subdivide and mount our grey scales to show new interactions, particularly between graduating and non-graduating greys, and vice versa.

Color intensity -- brightness

After the study of "Lighter or Darker" and with some training
in gradation studies, one can expect to come
to an agreement on different light intensities.

However, when it comes to color intensity (brightness),
occasionally one may find agreement among a few people
but hardly within a large group such as a class.

As "gentlemen prefer blondes," so everyone has preference for certain colors
and prejudices against others. This applies to color combinations as well.
It seems good that we are of different tastes.
As it is with people in our daily life, so it is with color.
We change, correct, or reverse our opinions about colors, and this change
of opinion may shift forth and back.

Therefore, we try to recognize our preferences and our aversions --
what colors dominate in our work; what colors, on the other hand,
are rejected, disliked, or of no appeal. Usually a special effort
in using disliked colors ends with our falling in love with them.

The exercise in color intensity consists of sorting
all possible shades and tints within a hue. From these is chosen
the most typical hue (the bluest blue, the greenest green, etc.)
and it is placed within the group accordingly.

VI 1 color appears as 2 -- looking like the reversed grounds

Having presented, in the previous problem, a very detailed explanation
of a step-by-step method of teaching and learning, the following problem
permits a briefer description.

With the first exercise in color interaction we make
        1 color look like 2, or, what means the same,
        3 colors look like 4. The next step is to make
        3 colors look like 2, or, describing it as in the previous task,
        1 color is to show 2 faces which refer to the 2 colors
        of the reversed grounds,
        or, the changed color is to echo the 2 changing ones.

After showing a few examples, the task of producing similar effects
is introduced with the question:
        Which color will play simultaneously the roles
        of the 2 colors of the 2 reciprocal grounds?

The first class exhibition of preliminary solutions shows that most of the
trial colors selected appear closer to one ground than to the other.

However, when one tries to find a color that is equally close
or equally distant from both grounds, one will discover that
even a large collection of color paper (even that of the entire class)
may not provide the fitting tone.

Then, instead of pushing the in-between color to one or the other side,
we must consider changing 1 or both of the grounds, either moving
closer to or more distant from the in-between color. (See diagram.)

After repeated trials it must be concluded that the only fitting color
is the one which is topologically in the middle of the colors
of the 2 grounds.

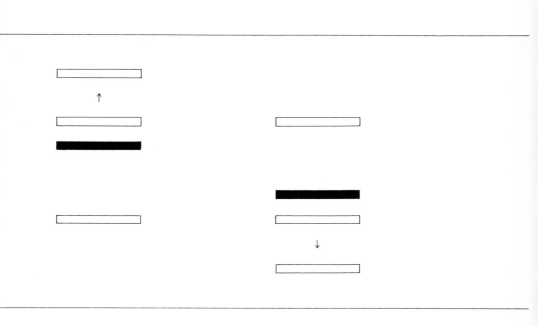

The task is to find this middle color.

This is relatively easy when the 2 grounds are of the same hue,
as with a lighter and a darker green ground,
or with a lighter and a darker violet ground..

It is a more challenging task to find the middle color
between 2 different hues
but it is particularly interesting when the 2 grounds
are of opposing (complementary) colors.

VII   2 different colors look alike -- subtraction of color

The fact that one and the same color can perform many different roles
is well known and is consciously applied.

Less well known is the possibility in the previous exercise
of giving a color the look of reversed grounds.

Still more exciting is the next task, the reverse of the first:
to make 2 different colors look alike.

In the first exercise it was learned that the more different
the grounds, the stronger is their changing influence.

It has been seen that color differences are caused by 2 factors:
by hue and by light, and in most cases by both at the same time.

Recognizing this, one is able to "push" light and/or hue,
by the use of contrasts, away from their first appearance
toward the opposite qualities.
Since this amounts virtually to adding opposite qualities,
it follows that one might achieve parallel effects
by subtracting those qualities not desired.

This new experience can be achieved first by observing
3 small samples of 3 reds on a white ground.
They will appear first of all -- red.

Then when the 3 reds are placed on a ground of another red
their differences, which are differences of hue as well as of light,
will become more obvious.

Third, when placed on a red ground equal to 1 of the 3 samples,
only 2 of the reds will "show," and the lost one is absorbed -- subtracted.
Repeated similar experiments with adjacent colors will show
that any ground subtracts its own hue from colors which it carries
and therefore influences.

Additional experiments with light colors on light grounds
and dark colors on dark grounds prove that the light of a ground
subtracts in the same way that its hue does.

From this, it follows that any diversion among colors
in hue as well as in light-dark relationship
can be reduced if not obliterated visually on grounds
of equal qualities.

Such studies provide a broad training in analytical comparison
and usually evoke surprising results, leading the student
to an intense study of color.

VIII Why color deception? -- after-image, simultaneous contrast

For a better understanding of why colors read differently
from what they really (physically) are, we show now
the cause of most color illusions.
(See Plates VIII -- 2.)

First: In order to prepare for the second part of this demonstration, cut out in
red and white color paper 2 equal circles (of ca. 3-inch diameter)
and mark their centers with a small black dot.

Then paste them -- horizontally related -- the red circle to
the left and the white one to the right, on the blackboard or
a piece of black paper or black cardboard, ca. 10 inches high and
20 inches long, with about equal amounts of black before, between,
and after the two circles.

Now, by staring steadily at the marked center of the red
circle (up to half a minute) one soon discovers how difficult
it is to keep the eye fixed on a point. After a while,
moon-sickle shapes appear, moving along the circle's
periphery. In spite of this, one must continue to focus on
the red center point in order to assure the desired experience.

Suddenly, one shifts the focus to the center of the white circle.
Then from the class one usually hears noises which indicate
surprise or astonishment. This happens because all normal eyes
suddenly see green or blue-green instead of white. This green
is the complementary color of red or red-orange.

The phenomenon of seeing green (in this case) instead of white
is called after-image, or simultaneous contrast.

Second: On the left are yellow circles of equal size which touch
          each other and which fill out a white square.
          On the right is an empty white square of the same size.
          Each is on a black ground.

          After staring for half a minute at the left square,
          one shifts the focus suddenly to the right square. Here one experiences
          a very different after-image. Instead of seeing
          the complement of the yellow circles (blue), diamond shapes
          are seen -- the leftover shapes of the circles -- in yellow.
          This illusion is a double and thus reversed after-image,
          sometimes called contrast reversal.

A plausible explanation:

One theory maintains that the nerve ends on the human retina (rods and cones)
are tuned to receive any of the 3 primary colors (red, yellow,
or blue), which constitute all colors.

Staring at red will fatigue the red-sensitive parts, so that with
a sudden shift to white (which again consists of red, yellow, and blue),
only the mixture of yellow and blue occurs. And this is green,
the complement of red.

The fact that the after-image or simultaneous contrast
is a psycho-physiological phenomenon should prove
that no normal eye, not even the most trained one, is foolproof
against color deception.
He who claims to see colors independent of their illusionary changes
fools only himself, and no one else.

IX Color mixture in paper -- illusion of transparence

It is obvious that in working with color paper there is no way
of mixing the colors mechanically, as paint and pigment permit,
and as they invite one to do on a palette or in a container.

Though this may first appear as a handicap, it is actually a challenge
to study color mixture in our imagination, that is, so to say,
with closed eyes.

Starting with the simple and well-known fact that blue and yellow
when mixed produce green, a blue and yellow are selected
and held next to each other. One tries to imagine what kind of green
would result from a mixture of these 2 colors.
Then a paper is selected appropriate to this imagined mixture.

In order to find out whether the "thought-out" mixture is acceptable --
believable -- convincing -- the 3 colors (2 "color parents" and
1 "color descendant") are placed in 3 equal rectangles as follows:

Blue horizontally (1), green vertically (2)
so that its upper part overlaps the blue. The yellow is put on top
of the green (3), so that its top edge coincides with the bottom edge of
the blue.

In such placement, the green will be the "in-between" of the other colors
and thus their mixture.

After the class has found several believable mixtures, these are collected
for an exhibition (most practically, on the floor) and the most convincing ones
are selected. Some are usually more successful than others. The class states
their merits and shortcomings and suggests possible corrections and improvements.

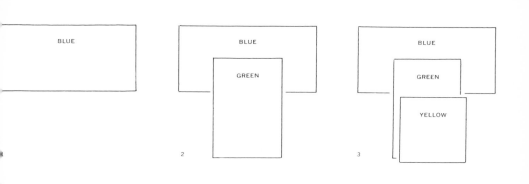

By means of the exhibition, the students will be reminded that there are many blues and many yellows, and will conclude that there are innumerable mixtures descending from them. It is obvious that any 2 colors can produce many mixtures.

In addition to the illusion of mixture, another deception will be recognized -- that, in an illusionary mixture in paper, 1 color seems to show through the other. The "mixture" paper, therefore, loses its opacity and appears transparent or translucent.

In order to make the eye read this double illusion of mixture and of transparence, the colors must be placed in overlapping shapes.

In the drawing on page 26 the hatched parts belong to each of the overlapping shapes and are therefore the logical place for the mixture.

After simple mixtures, such as blue and yellow producing green -- red and blue producing violet -- black and white producing grey -- less common pairs, such as pink and ochre, present a further challenge.

For a more intensive experience, keep the area of the mixture larger than those of the 2 mixing ones.

If we name 2 mixture parents A and B, and their mixture C,
then our first task is to find C's, which are mixtures of A and B,
another task will be   "   "   B's conditioned by   A " C,
or, a third task,   "   "   A's   "   "   B " C.

This invites one to draw conclusions backward, that is, to guess --
from a mixture and 1 mixture parent -- the other mixture parent.

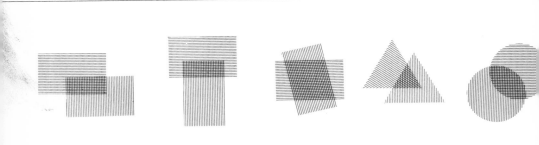

X   Factual mixtures -- additive and subtractive

Though the color class (as a rule) abstains from the use of colorants
(meaning pigments and paints) for reasons explained before,
the color studies in paper are related to the actual use of paint
as often as possible.

Therefore, after the introductory studies of mixture as illusion,
factual mixing is analyzed. There are 2 kinds of physical mixture:

a)   Direct mixture of projected light,
b)   Indirect mixture of reflected light.

a)   Color light, or direct color, probably is most familiar
          through its practical application in theater and advertising.
          The scientific analysis of the physical qualities (wave length, etc.)
          is not the problem of the colorist; it is the concern of the physicist.
          When he mixes his colors, he projects them on a screen,
          1 on top of or overlapping the other.
          In any such mixture where there is overlapping,
          it will be obvious that every one of these mixtures
          is lighter than any of the mixture parents.
          By means of a prismatic lens, the physicist easily demonstrates
          that the color spectrum of the rainbow is a dispersion of the white sunlight.
          With this he proves also that the sum of all colors in light is white.
          This demonstrates an additive mixture.

b)   When pigment or paint is mixed on a palette or in a container
          it is seen by the eye as reflected light.
          This mixing will never result in white as the sum of colors.
          On the contrary, the more color that is mixed, the more the mixture approaches
          a dark grey leaning toward black. This we call subtractive mixture.
          Also, the psychologist, who mixes colors of reflecting colorants
          optically on the rotating wheel, is not able to arrive at mixtures
          lighter than the lighter color parent of the mixture.

          As optical mixture usually means less loss of light
          than mechanical mixture, the psychologist's sum of all his colors
          normally approaches a middle grey instead of the dark grey of the painter.

The conclusion is: mixtures gain light only in direct color, as in (a), whereas mixtures of reflected colors lose light, as in (b).

Though direct color or color light normally is not the medium of the colorist, examples of this effect should be indicated. Additive and subtractive mixtures should be made in appropriate studies in transparence illusions. These will provide a preparatory training for studies to follow.

For the sake of simplicity and to avoid difficult complications, these mixtures should be done in 1 thin color mixing preferably with white (or black), and then reversing the first study.

Sample arrangements:

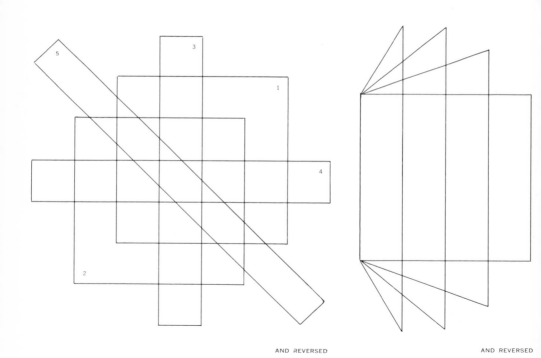

AND REVERSED   AND REVERSED

XI   Transparence and space-illusion

Color boundaries and plastic action

A study of color mixture in paper leads to 3 important discoveries.

First, under normal conditions, a subtractive mixture is not as light
as the lighter of the color parents nor as dark as the darker one.
Furthermore, the mixture is reciprocally neither higher nor lower
in color intensity than the color parents.

Second, a mixture depends upon the proportion in which colors are mixed.
Varying amounts of blue and yellow, for instance, define the character
of a green. This indicates a possible predominance of 1 color parent.

Third, when 1 color is read as appearing above or below another
in the transparence studies, a third deception is recognized -- space-illusion.

This leads to the next task:
To produce different illusionary mixtures which derive from 1 pair
of parent colors. If the parents are again a blue and a yellow,
some greens will be found with yellow dominance
and others with blue dominance. With more mixing experience
it will become apparent that the nearness of a mixture to one side
(let us say yellow) necessitates distance from the opposite side
(in this case blue).

After having found several mixtures of different pairs of parent colors,
we then try to find the most significant and the most difficult mixture
-- the middle mixture. Topographically, this middle mixture demands
precise placement, and therefore additional means of measure are necessary.

Since the middle mixture presupposes equidistance from the color parents,
it therefore depends equally upon the absence of any predominance
of the color parents.

Here, the following diagrams may be helpful:

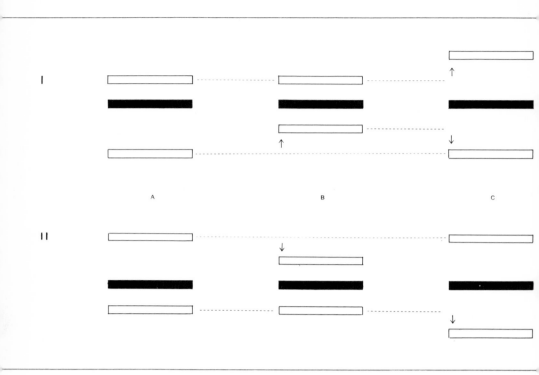

I   A   B   C

II

Of the 3 bars in each diagram, the black bar
(which appears either above, or below, or in the middle) represents
an in-between color, the mixture in question; that is, the one
to be "equidistant" from the accompanying white bars.
The latter represent possible color parents for a color mixture.
The upper bar represents a lighter (higher) color,
and the lower bar represents a deeper (heavier) color.

In Iᴀ the mixture line is nearer to the upper line, and is therefore too light;
in IIᴀ the opposite happens. The middle color-to-be is nearer to the
lower bar and consequently is too dark. For the necessary corrections
in Iᴀ, we must look for a lower (darker) middle, and in IIᴀ for a higher
(lighter) middle.

Unfortunately, those higher and lower tones are often not available.
In such cases, we should try to adjust the outer (upper or lower) colors

-- instead of the middle color -- in order to exercise another way
of correct placement.

Thus, in Iʙ the lower bar is lifted from the dotted line,
e.g. a lighter color is chosen; in IIʙ the upper bar is lowered.
In c similar changes take place but in an
opposite direction from ʙ. Comparing groups ʙ and c will
demonstrate that correct arrangements may become closer to or more distant
from the middle color.

Such efforts forth and back in our search for a middle color --
to be specific, for a middle placement -- provide through
continued comparison a thorough visual training:
"thinking in situations."

Besides an explanation of the above diagrams on the blackboard,
a physical demonstration in space may clarify this further.
When discussing the first trial studies, exhibited on the floor
with the students standing around them, 2 hands held horizontally
1 above the other may act as the 2 outer colors.
And a third hand held between them may demonstrate various possibilities
of color selection and placement, either by moving the hand indicating
the middle color up or down, or by moving the outer hands up
and/or down, singly or together.

With a more developed sensitivity for mixtures, it will be discovered
that distance, nearness, and equidistance between colors
can be recognized through the boundaries between the mixture and the mixture parents.

By exercising comparison and distinction of color boundaries, a new and
important measure is gained for the reading of the plastic action of color,
that is, for the spatial organization of color.
Since softer boundaries disclose nearness implying connection,
harder boundaries indicate distance, separation.

In both interpretations colors are placed above or below each other,
or in front of or behind each other. They are read as here and there,
as over, and beyond there, and therefore in space.

All this seems to change with colors producing middle mixtures. Sometimes

they appear as if meeting within a 2-dimensional plane; at other times
they can be read -- interchangeably -- as higher or lower than the mixture.

Thus, with a middle mixture all boundaries are equally soft or hard.
As a consequence, a middle mixture appears frontal, as a color by itself.
This is comparable to the reading of any symmetrical order
and the middle mixture will behave unspatially,
unless its own shape, or surrounding shapes, decides differently.

(See Plate XI -- 3.)

Such a study, or a similar recognition, in my opinion, led Cézanne
to his unique and new articulation in painting. He was the first
to develop color areas which produce both distinct and indistinct endings
-- areas connected and unconnected -- areas with and without boundaries --
as means of plastic organization.

And, in order to prevent evenly painted areas from looking flat and frontal,
he used emphasized borders sparingly, mainly where he needed
a spatial separation from adjacent color areas.

XII Optical mixture -- after-image revised

XIII The Bezold Effect

In contrast to after-image, so far the main concern of our studies, here
is another very different color illusion called "optical mixture."
Instead of 2 (or more) colors changing each other, "pulling" or "pushing"
each other into different appearances (toward both greater difference and greater
similarity), here 2 colors (or more), perceived simultaneously, are seen
combined and thus merged into 1 new color. In this process, the 2
original colors are first annulled and made invisible, and then replaced by
a substitute called optical mixture.

From the Impressionist painters we have learned that they never presented, let us say,
green by itself. Instead of using green paint mixed mechanically from yellow
and blue, they applied yellow and blue unmixed in small dots, so that they
became mixed only in our perception -- as an impression. That the dots
mentioned were small indicates that this effect depends on size and on distance.

The discovery of the mixing of colors in our perception led in the last
century not only to the new painting technique of the Impressionists, and
particularly of the Pointillists, but also to the invention of new photomechanical
reproduction techniques, the 3- and 4-color process for paintings, and the
halftone process for black-and-white pictures. In the first case, 3 or 4
color plates subdivided into tiny printing dots mix to innumerable color
shades and tints. In the second case, a plate for black also subdivided by
a screen in tiny dots mixes with the white paper in just as innumerable
tones of white -- grey -- black.

There is a special kind of optical mixture, the Bezold Effect, named after its
discoverer, Wilhelm von Bezold (1837–1907). He recognized
this effect when searching for a method through which he could change the
color combinations of his rug designs entirely by adding or changing 1 color only.
Apparently, there is so far no clear recognition of the optical-
perceptual conditions involved.

XIV Color intervals and transformation

The tune of "Good morning to you" consists of 4 tones. It can be sung
in a high soprano, a low basso, and in all in-between voices, as well as
on many levels and in many keys. It can be played on innumerable instruments.

In all possible ways of performance, this melody will keep its character
and it will be recognized instantly.

Why? The intervals of the 4 tones, that is, their acoustical
constellation (again comparable with a topographic relationship),
remains the same.

Although it is not common practice, one can also speak of intervals
between colors.
Colors and hues are defined, as are tones in music, by wave length.

Any color (shade or tint) always has 2 decisive characteristics:
color intensity (brightness) and light intensity (lightness).
Therefore, color intervals also have this double-sidedness, this duality.

As has been stated before, after some training one might easily agree
on light relationship, that is, which of 2 colors is lighter
and which is darker. However, there is rarely agreement on color intensity,
that is, which among a number of reds is the reddest red.
For this reason the interval transformation exercise is concerned mainly
with light intensity.

To prepare a basic exercise in color transformation, combine
4 equal squares of different colors to make 1 larger square.
Within this grouping of 4 squares, the lighter will differentiate
from the heavier, darker color. Therefore, the squares will connect
with each other or separate according to contrast and affinity,
as vertical, horizontal, or diagonal pairs, or as a trio forming
an angle, embracing or opposing a fourth square. (See diagrams.)

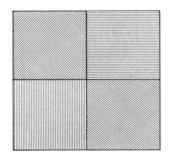 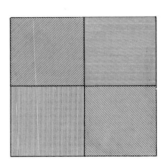

The task is to transfer these specific relationships to a higher or lower key
within 2 or more groups of equally large rectangles. Of course,
if the first group contains the darkest color available, one cannot go lower.
Similarly, the lightest white would not permit any transference to
a higher key.

It is rarely possible to retain the first 4 rectangles selected.
Frequently it will be impossible to find 4 colors equally raised
or lowered when compared with the original set. If so, the original set
should be changed in order to transfer more successfully.

In a successful study, both groups should show equal relationships
in equal placement, as a constellation. Then, as with the study of
varying mixtures, the boundaries between the 4 rectangles
will also appear similar in both groups.

Again, the aim of this exercise is not to present a pleasant, perhaps harmonious look,
but to present a study aiming at one distinct relationship --
parallel intervals.

How do we prove such similarity, such parallelism?
As has been learned from gradation studies done at the beginning, it is
poor "psychological engineering" to present the gradation steps
unconnected, that is, separated by black lines. Similarly, in the transformation
exercise it is hard to compare the boundaries within the
original group of 4 rectangles with the raised or lowered boundaries in
the second, separated group.

The only way in which the 2 groups can be compared easily and accurately
is to superimpose 1 group on the other.

For this purpose we cut from the center of the first group
a small rectangle and exchange it with an equally shaped and placed
small rectangle of the second group. (See diagrams below.)

Immediately, the superimposed rectangles will show
whether the stepping up or down within 1 group corresponds
with the stepping in the other. A further comparison should be made
between each small rectangle and the larger group beneath it.
The sample studies will also show that the boundaries provide
an important means of comparison.

Usually, as shown, a lower color tetrachord is transferred
to a higher key, or opposite; one may also break with habit and
try to make a low color constellation still lower, or a high one
still higher.

By keeping the stepping -- up or down -- small, a special effect of
transparence is achieved called film color, to be described in Chapter XVII.

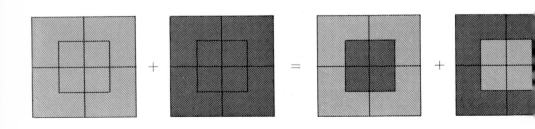

XV   The middle mixture again -- intersecting colors

Our studies of illusionary transparence have shown how difficult it is
to find middle mixture.

A true middle mixture is distinguished by being equidistant
-- in light and in hue --
from either mixture parent.

Unfortunately, for an untrained eye, it is hard to recognize
such equidistance.
We have seen that the color boundaries between the mixing color
and the mixed one have proved to be helpful measures.

The purpose of the new problem, intersecting colors,
is to show and to produce a certain constellation
by which even an untrained eye will recognize
within a mixture not only the constituents
but also their respective amounts within that mixture.

For an initial experience in this direction
find 3 equally large sheets of 1 red in 3 shades,
a light red, the same red darker, and the almost always elusive
middle mixture of these reds. Or, if not available in red,
take any other color providing a lighter, a middle, and
a darker shade or tint. (See diagrams, next page.)

Place them adjacent to one another,
with the lighter red to the left and overlapped by the edge of the middle red;
then place the dark red on top of the middle red, allowing only a narrow strip
of the middle red (about ¼ inch wide) to remain visible.

Then, very slowly, pull the dark sheet to the right,
gradually making the narrow strip of the middle red wider.

By staring at the middle red, observe that the wider it grows, the more it appears
not as 1 but as 2 colors, becoming lighter and lighter
at the right edge, and, at the same time, darker and darker
at the left edge.

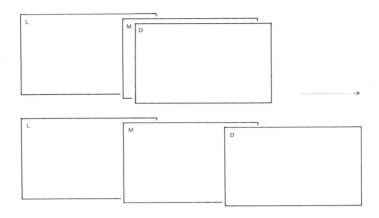

By doing this repeatedly, it becomes obvious that the middle color
plays the role of both mixture parents, presenting them
in reversed placement.

Repeating this experience with other colors will show that
in a true middle mixture the mixture parents will appear
in equal amounts.

In most cases, however, the larger amount of 1 of the 2 colors
reveals its predominance.

Such exercises are exciting as well as revealing, particularly
when extended to different and opposing colors.

These exercises remind us that the basic after-image presentation,
the simultaneous contrast, is the cause of all color deception.

Whereas the first measuring of middle mixtures led us
to space illusion through connecting and separating boundaries,
this direct reading of the mixture constituents leads us
to a new deception: an illusion of volume.

It is an effect we have seen in the channelings of the Doric column
and is called a fluting effect. (See Plate XV -- 2.)

XVI Color juxtaposition -- harmony -- quantity

Harmony

Color systems usually lead to the conclusion
that certain constellations within a system provide color harmony.
They indicate that this is mainly the aim and the end
of color combination, of color juxtaposition.

As harmony and harmonizing is also a concern of music, so
a parallelism of effect between tone combinations and color combinations
seems unavoidable and appropriate. Although
a comparison of composed colors with composed tones is very challenging,
it should be mentioned that, while it can be helpful,
it is often misleading.

This is because different basic conditions of these media result in
different behavior.

Tones appear placed and directed predominantly in time from <u>before</u>
to <u>now</u> to <u>later</u>.

Their juxtaposition in a musical composition is perceived
within a prescribed sequence only. Vertically, so to say,
1 tone, or several simultaneously,
sound for a varying but restricted length of time.
Horizontally, the tones follow each other,
perhaps not in a straight line, but of necessity in a prescribed order
and only in 1 direction -- forward.
Tones heard earlier fade, and those farther back disappear, vanish.
We do not hear them backward.

Colors appear connected predominantly in space. Therefore,
as constellations they can be seen in any direction and
at any speed. And as they remain, we can return to them repeatedly
and in many ways.

This remaining and not remaining, or vanishing and not vanishing,
shows only 1 essential difference between the fields of tone
and color.

The accuracy of perception in one field is matched
by the durability of retention in the other, demonstrating
a curious reversal in visual and auditory memory.

Tone juxtapositions can be defined by their acoustical relationship
and thus measured precisely by wave length.

Consequently, a graphic registration of tones in musical composition
has been developed.

Color, also, can be measured, at least to some extent,
and particularly so when it is presented as direct color --
as the physicist registers it, by optical wave length.

Reflected color, however, coming from paint and pigment
-- our main medium -- is much more difficult to define.

When analyzed with an electrical spectrograph
reflected color shows that it contains all visible wave lengths.
Therefore, any reflected color -- not just white --
consists of all other colors.

This many-sided relationship between colors is clearly visible
in the plates of a 4-color reproduction, when singly shown,
because each of the 4 plates, although presenting only 1 color,
shows a complete picture.

Color, when practically applied, not only appears in uncountable
shades and tints, but is additionally characterized
by shape and size, by recurrence and placement, and so on, of which
particularly shape and size are not directly applicable
to tones.

All this may signify why any color composition naturally defies
such diagrammatic registration as notation in music
and choreography in dance.

With regard to constellation, tone intervals, such as third, fifth, and octave,
differentiate exact vertical distance. We say "vertical" probably because
tones are described as low and high.
Slide deflections (aberrations), such as in flat and sharp,
remain equally precise.
Color terms which could be considered parallel to tone intervals
are complementaries, split complementaries, triads, tetrads, and octads.
Though these characterize distance and constellation within color systems,
their deflections, such as incomplete triads and incomplete tetrads,
indicate that their measure is only arbitrary.

Significantly, complementaries, though they are the basic color contrast
or interval, are topographically quite vague.

In principle, a complementary is a color accompanied by its after-image.

However, the complement of a specific color, when placed
in different systems, will look different.

Similarly, a triad or tetrad of one system will hardly fit
into another system.

Usually, illustrations of harmonic color constellations which derive
from authoritative systems look pleasant, beautiful, and thus convincing.
But it should not be overlooked that they are usually presented in a
most theoretical and least practicable manner, because normally
all harmony members appear in the same quantity and the same shape,
as well as in the same number (just once) and sometimes even in similar
light intensity.
Such outer equalization may unify them, but at the expense
of the more important inner relatedness -- namely, as color only.

When applied in practice, these harmony sets appear changed.
In addition to quantity, form, and recurrence,
wider aspects exert still more changing influences.
These are:

>   Changed and changing light -- and, even worse,
>   several simultaneous lights;
>   reflection of lights and of colors;
>   direction and sequence of reading;

presentation in varying materials;
constant or altering juxtaposition of related
and unrelated objects.

With these and other visual displacements, it should not be a surprise
that the sympathetic effect of the original "ideal" color combination
often appears changed, lost, and reversed.

Observe the interior and exterior, the furniture and textile decoration
following such color schemes, as well as commercialized color "suggestions"
for innumerable do-it-yourselves.

Our conclusion: we may forget for a while those rules of thumb
of complementaries, whether complete or "split," and of triads and
tetrads as well.
They are worn out.

Second, no mechanical color system is flexible enough
to precalculate the manifold changing factors, as named before,
in a single prescribed recipe.

Good painting, good coloring, is comparable to good cooking.
Even a good cooking recipe demands tasting and repeated tasting
while it is being followed.
And the best tasting still depends on a cook with taste.

By giving up preference for harmony,
we accept dissonance to be as desirable as consonance.

In searching for new color organization -- color design --
we have come to think that quantity, intensity, or weight, as principles of study,
can lead similarly to illusions, to new relationships, to different measurements,
to other systems, as do transparence, space, and intersection.

Besides a balance through color harmony, which is comparable
to symmetry, there is equilibrium possible between
color tensions, related to a more dynamic asymmetry.

Again: knowledge and its application is not our aim;
instead, it is flexible imagination, discovery, invention -- taste.

With this study of color effects, that is, of color deception,
a special interest in quantity -- amount as well as recurrence --
has developed.

Quantity

Although quantity and quality often are considered disparate, in art and
music they appear closely related. We may even hear, "Quantity
is a quality," because here quantity not only designates amounts,
as of weight or number, but also is a means of underlining,
of pronouncement, and a means of equilibrium, of balance.

One who particularly recognized the latter was Schopenhauer.
When he tried to improve Goethe's 6-part color circle -- to Goethe's dismay --
he changed the previous presentation of 6 equal areas to decidedly
different quantities.

Thus yellow, the lightest color, appears in the smaller amount,
and its opposite, violet, as the darkest, in the largest amount.
He first allotted 3 equal thirds of a color ring to the 3 pairs
of opposites -- yellow & violet -- blue & orange -- red & green.
Second, he subdivided those thirds, for the same order of pairs,
in $\frac{1}{4} + \frac{3}{4}$ -- $\frac{1}{3} + \frac{2}{3}$ -- $\frac{1}{2} + \frac{1}{2}$. These figures
in fractions of 12ths (relatively 36ths) are proportionate to
$3 : 9$ -- $4 : 8$ -- $6 : 6$ equal parts.
When seen in a color circle, from yellow around to green, they present
the following quantities: $3 : 4 : 6 : 9 : 8 : 6$.

The 2 basic quantity questions, how much and how often,
distinguish 2 kinds of quantity:
1 of size -- extension in area -- and
1 of recurrence -- extension in number.
Both measurements concern predominance and emphasis.
They establish weight in space -- and weight in time.

Such considerations are both the source and result of our quantity studies
in which 4 colors usually appear in 4 different juxtapositions,
so different that all 4 studies appear as unrelated as possible.

And thus they present changes in climate or temperature,
in tempo or rhythm -- that is, changes of atmosphere or mood,
so that the factual contents (the same 4 colors) are hidden or, better,
hardly recognizable.

To use a theatrical parallel:
A set of 4 colors is to be considered -- singly as "actors,"
together as "cast." They are to be presented in 4 different
arrangements -- as "performances."

Although they remain unchanged in hue and light, in "character,"
and appear in an unchanging outer frame, the "stage,"
they are to produce 4 different "scenes" or "plays,"
each to be so different that one and the same set of colors will be seen as
4 different sets, presented by 4 different casts.

And all this can be achieved mainly through changes in quantity
which result in shifts of dominance, of recurrence, and consequently
of placement.

The essential question: which group of colors is ready to lose
its identity as a cast?

A parallel question: which distribution of appearance
(quantities of space, time, and weight) protects, disguises
recognition of the same color cast?

Such quantity studies have taught us to believe that, independent
of harmony rules, any color "goes" or "works" with any other color,
presupposing that their quantities are appropriate.
We feel fortunate that so far there are no comprehensive rules
for such aims.

Here we may point to a discovery made by a few contemporary painters,
that the increase in amount of a color -- not merely in size of canvas --
visually reduces distance. As a consequence, it often produces nearness --
meaning intimacy -- and respect.

XVII Film color and volume color -- 2 natural effects

Usually, we think of an apple as being red.
This is not the same red as that of a cherry or tomato.
A lemon is yellow and an orange is like its name.
Bricks vary from beige to yellow to orange,
and from ochre to brown to deep violet.
Foliage appears in innumerable shades of green.
In all these cases the colors named are surface colors.

In a very different way, distant mountains appear uniformly blue,
no matter whether covered
with green trees or consisting of earth and rocks.
The sun is glaring white in daytime, but is full red at sunset.
The white ceilings of houses surrounded by lawns or the white-painted
eaves of a roof on a sunny day appear in bright green, which is
reflected from the grass on the ground.
All these cases present film colors.

They appear as a thin, transparent, translucent layer between the eye
and an object, independent of the object's surface color.

For a very different color effect compare the coffee in a cup with the
coffee in the stem of a percolator or with the coffee in a silex glass.
It is easy to discover that, though all 3 containers hold the same
coffee, the containers show this coffee in 3 different browns:
lightest in the stem, darker in the cup, darkest in the silex glass.

In the same way, tea will look lighter in a spoon than in a cup.
Here we are dealing with volume color,
which exists and is perceived in 3-dimensional fluids.

The water of a swimming pool with blue walls will look dyed with blue
because of diffused reflection. Observing the white or blue steps
within the water, we will discover that with each step down
the blue of the water increases progressively, which presents a true
volume color effect.
In Chapter XX it will be explained in what proportion the blue increases.

On the other hand, milk remains more or less the same white,
no matter whether seen in a small or large container.
Ink and oil paint behave in a similar way.
This demonstrates that only transparent fluids present volume color.

In practice, most water colors are volume colors; several layers
on top of each other increase the darkness, weight, and intensity of a color.
Many aquarelles by Paul Klee demonstrate this.
The reverse effect of increased lightness is seen in fingerpaintings.

In contrast to water colors, such media as oil paint, gouache, and pastel
produce surface color. In most cases these paints do not change
to any extent when applied in several layers.

A new medium with volume color effect is a photosensitive glass
developed by Corning Glass Works. With increased exposure
to certain rays, the translucent opalescent white within the glass increases.
This results in a darkening of the whites with light passing through,
but in a whiter white in reflected light.

A similar effect can be achieved in tracing paper. By looking
through several layers against the light, the paper becomes darker.
However, the same layers seen from the direction of the light will appear whiter.
Since film color is not the result of physiological or psychological transformation,
it is a physical phenomenon.
Both film color and volume color might be considered tricks of nature.

Free studies -- a challenge to imagination

The previous chapters deal mostly with tasks to be solved as
class problems. Through them, all class members work in 1
direction only. This means they compete for the solution of
1 given problem at a time -- that of a single color effect.
Although the solutions may differ considerably, and especially so
in their presentation, the work of the whole class appears unified.

Such studies aim at the development of observation, of differentiation.
And this is particularly so through an inevitable constant comparison
going on from student to student. As a consequence, these studies
permit hardly any self-expression.

Thus, after such systematic exercises, a need for independent work arises,
and free studies are encouraged. With them one may play with colors
as one pleases, independent of exercises, independent of teachers
and of other students.

Whereas the systematic problems occupy most of the class time and
are finished afterward, the free studies are mostly homework, although
they accompany the systematic studies almost from the beginning
through the whole course.

The measure for evaluation of free studies is color relatedness.
This means color juxtaposition in which color exists for color's sake,
and therefore appears autonomous, and not merely as accompaniment
to form, to shape.

Whether something "has color" or not is as hard to define verbally as are
such questions as "what is music" or "what is musical."

The reproductions of free studies (see Plate XVIII -- 1) may indicate
that the possibilities are endless. Since showing such samples may present
a handicap, one might stimulate a beginning with thematic suggestions.

Experience has taught that pairs of contrasts
invoke a more distinct "meaning" and a more precise "reading."

First themes:
gay -- sad   young -- old   major -- minor

More daring:
bright -- dull   early -- late   active -- passive

These themes easily evoke discussions without end, since verbal reactions
to the associations with color differ vastly from person to person.

Another stimulation is the problem of free studies in colors of a limited range.
This means a restricted palette with, for instance, only contrasting
or only adjacent colors, with selections of preferred or of disliked colors.

Any of these cases may aim for concord or discord.

Such and other restrictions usually result from a personal choice.
More revealing, though harder to do, is the submission to selections
by others. To work with the preference of others, to subordinate
to someone else's palette or instrumentation, should be not only permitted
but encouraged.

All this is to promote competition. And with that comes evaluation
through comparison, which in the end means judgment.
A strong challenge to a class is to work with 3 or 4 given colors
selected by a teacher or student. This and a continued use of disliked colors
will teach that preferences and dislikes -- as in life so with color
-- usually result from prejudices, from lack of experience and insight.

Stripes -- restricted juxtaposition

The first attempts to produce "free studies" usually result in the dominance
of form or shape -- and often very pronounced -- over color.

This means, in most cases, that the outlines of the colors predominate.
And, as visually the loudest, they are noticed first. Thus color appears
of secondary interest, or only as accompaniment of shape.

And this remains the normal result so long as the most decisive difference
between color in paper and color in paint is not clearly recognized:
colors in paper always consist of outspoken flat areas
which present even colors reaching precisely from edge to edge.
And the edges, by their very nature as uninterrupted endless contours,
again advocate shape first.

For this reason, it is advisable to recommend torn papers for the beginning
as they ordinarily offer looser and freer edges
than cut papers.
More experience will lead to other means of softening or hardening
color boundaries: smaller or greater contrasts of hue or of light;
elemental or complex shapes; curved, straight, broken, or dotted lines.

By combining colors exclusively in stripes -- that is,
in stretched, narrow rectangles, all of the same length, varying
only in width, and touching each other in full length --
we are led to overlook their rather equal shapes and to consider them
almost shapeless.

As to placement of the stripes in horizontal or vertical direction,
the latter appears more practicable. In a left-right and
therefore sideward contact, color interaction usually
is more easily comprehensible than within an up-down connection.
And with this, our reading, connecting, grouping, and separating
of the color stripes is easier.

The first task is to organize a large number of color stripes --
all narrow, of varying width but equal length, all vertical and touching
each other, presenting only 4 colors -- and only later to choose more or fewer colors.

The aim is to find an order in which, again relatively,
all 4 colors are equally important, or, respectively, equally unimportant.
In other words, none of the colors dominates.
We say "relatively" in consideration of our individual attitude toward color,
of our differing preferences for certain colors, and our dislikes of others.

With a continuous alternation and recurrence of the 4 colors
innumerable combinations and arrangements are possible.
And the more they vary, the more they invite one to follow and to alter,

with a constant change in connecting and dividing, overlapping and intersecting
of seemingly many more than 4 colors.

We may consider such calculated juxtaposition as a symbol
of community spirit, of "live and let live," of "equal rights for all,"
of mutual respect.

We should also encourage working with very different colors,
so that light and color intensity may compete with
and balance each other.

Such studies in stripes will readily remind us of textiles,
and we may read and interpret them as fabrics of wool or cotton --
for various uses -- of various color climates: from new to old, young to old,
modern to old -- related to peoples, times, and periods.

The purpose is to stimulate again a reading of the meaning
of form, to invite verbal formulation of reaction to
our associations with climates in color.

The second problem in color stripes aims at different results:
dominance of 1 or more colors and broad areas is suggested;
and either coordination and/or subordination is permitted.

More freedom in the number and the choice of colors
and their extension and repetition is given.
But restrictions to equal height and vertical partitioning
remain, in order to avoid interference of form.

Whereas the first task has reminded us of striped textiles,
here one may think of walls which are subdivided for
structural, illusional, decorative purposes.

Though the second type of color studies in stripes
leads usually to a more broad and bright palette --
in a positive reaction to the first, more restricted task --
it will again prove more profitable to aim
with fewer means toward more action.

Fall leaf studies -- an American discovery

Nowhere in the world, it seems to us, is the autumn foliage as brilliant
in color as in the United States.

When leaves are collected, pressed, and dried -- eventually varnished,
even bleached, and sometimes also dyed or painted -- they provide
a most welcome enrichment of any color paper collection.

Collected in all varieties, in all possible shades of color
-- in large numbers for an easy exchange between students -- they are both
exciting to see and most stimulating to work with in free studies.

As studies show, these leaves work beautifully with color paper.
They add innumerable tints and shades, with modulations and shapes
that color papers do not have. They are used singly and in groups,
in parts and combined again, repeated and reversed. Always
keep in mind the color before the shape. Colorful leaves suit all
ways of play and imagination for all kinds of order and placement.
Therefore, they remain a favorite means of study.

Naturally, leaf studies are best done in their season, in autumn,
at other times with prepared, preserved leaves which, of course,
provide more subdued, less vivid colors.

As leaf studies are free studies (usually done as homework),
they are mentioned here under that title, as are studies in stripes.

XIX The Masters -- color instrumentation

It should be clear by now that our way of studying color
does not start with the past -- neither with works of the past
nor with its theories.

As we begin principally with the material, color itself,
and its action and interaction as registered in our minds,
we practice first and mainly a study of ourselves.

Thus, we replace looking backward by looking first at ourselves and
our surroundings, and replace retrospection with introspection.

Though our own development and our own work are closest to us,
we see and appreciate encouragement from achievements of the past,
and gratefully pay practical respect to their originators
as often as the opportunity arises.

To honor the masters creatively is to compete with their attitude
rather than with their results, to follow an artistic understanding
of tradition -- that is, to create, not to revive.

Therefore, in our study of the masters -- both past and present --
there is, beyond mere retrospection and above verbal analysis,
re-creating by re-performing
their selection and presentation of color,
their seeing and reading of color --
in other words, their giving a meaning to color.

Singing a tune and playing it on instruments --
even more, conducting several instruments --
provides more contact, more insight than merely hearing the tune.
So cooking, normally and naturally, teaches more than reading recipes.

As a conclusion, we transfer paintings by masters into color paper,
in order to identify their color instrumentation.

Our aim is not production of precise replicas
as copyists do in museums.

We try to give a general impression only as to climate, temperature,
aroma, or sound of their work -- not minute details.

The purpose of such study is neither to find out,
for instance, whether ultramarine or cobalt blue was used,
nor to register the factual content of the painter's palette.

It is another means of learning to develop
a sensitive and critical eye for color relatedness.

The result of our transformation of paintings into color paper
depends on several limitations. Naturally, in making them,
we depend on reproductions.

In 3- and 4-color halftones, all colors are represented as optical mixtures
of 3 or 4 standardized inks. These are mostly transparent,
mixing not only with each other
but also with the white paper underneath.
That is to say, such reproductions are physically already
of an absolutely different instrumentation.

The resulting false and misleading smoothness, even slickness or sweetness,
and the dramatized brightness of so-called high-key color reproduction
are easily and pleasantly counteracted and corrected by paper colors.
This is the result of the opacity or visual weight of paper colors,
and their varying density and volume.

As a rule, paintings transferred to color paper look painted;
they do not look printed.
In the case of a Van Gogh and a Soutine, we easily regain
the effect of dramatic execution.
And works of Matisse appear again as juxtaposition of flat color areas,
opaque as well as untextured.

With such studies we submit to formulations of the past
in order to provoke further comparisons
of different attitudes, temperaments, mentalities, and personalities --
all for the sake of continued self-criticism and self-evaluation.
This proclaims creative action ahead of retrospective reaction.

XX The Weber-Fechner Law -- the measure in mixture

In order to obtain a graduated scale of greys, M. E. Chevreul,
the author of the famous book "The Laws of Contrast of Colour,"
gave the following instructions (from the English translation of 1868,
page 5, paragraph 11):

> Upon a sheet of cardboard divided into ten stripes,
> each about a quarter of an inch broad,
> lay a uniform tint of India ink. As soon as it is dry,
> lay a second tint on all the stripes except the first.
> As soon as the second is dry, lay a third one
> on all the stripes except the first and second,
> and so on all the rest, so as to have
> ten flat tints gradually increasing
> in depth from the first to the last.

All this sounds quite convincing, so convincing that one wonders
whether anyone has ever doubted that the result would be as promised --
whether anyone has ever followed these instructions, including M. Chevreul
himself.

All this, of course, refers to volume color (see page 45) but,
most important, it also leads to a new insight into color mixture --
after an unavoidable surprise is recognized.

The surprise is that the gradual "increase in depth" promised above
does not appear -- as most people will expect -- in a succession of
equal steps. Nor, when mixing pigments, does an equal gradation appear
when an equal quantity of the same color is continually added.

In this case a continued application of such layers would
unavoidably lead to such a degree of decrease that the initial increase would
disappear in a final, unsurpassable, and unchanging saturation.

Analyzing Chevreul's method of applying one layer on top of another,
one recognizes not only an additive mixture with regard to color, but
also a subtractive mixture with regard to light.

More precisely, this demonstrates an arithmetical progression
in both directions -- and both are physical progressions only.

In the diagrams on page 56, this physical fact is presented
by a row of rising steps of equal height and width, the movement of which
follows a straight line.

As said before, and clearly shown in Klee's water colors, the rate of
increase gradually decreases. Therefore, the rise of the steps will be
less and less high. Consequently, the physically straight line of
direction becomes psychologically a curve, ending in a horizontal line
representing saturation, which ends both increase and decrease.

This leads to the question: what is necessary to produce a visually
even progression in mixture?

The answer was found by Weber (Wilhelm Eduard, 1804–91) and Fechner
(Gustav Theodor, 1801–87). It is formulated in the so-called Weber-Fechner Law:
The visual perception of an arithmetical progression depends upon a physical
geometric progression.

Explained in diagrams shown on the next page, this means:
If the first 2 steps measure 1 and 2 units in rise, then
step 3 is not only 1 unit more (that is, 3 in an arithmetical proportion),
but is twice as much (that is, 4 in a geometric
proportion). The successive steps then measure 8, 16, 32, 64 units.
Such increases describe an upward curve ending in a straight vertical line, meaning,
again, saturation.

However, the reading of such geometric increase will describe a straight line
in our mind. We think and "feel" that we read steps of equal height.

To demonstrate this surprising discrepancy between physical fact and psychic effect,
and, more important, to become convinced of it through one's own experience,
the following exercise is recommended:

On a white paper, layers of very light transparent coats of a very thin color
are placed on top of each other; first, as M. Chevreul suggests,

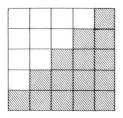
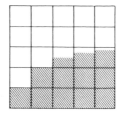

THIS PHYSICAL FACT   REDUCES TO   THIS PSYCHOLOGICAL EFFECT

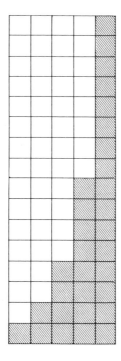

THIS PHYSICAL FACT   PRODUCES   THIS PSYCHOLOGICAL EFFECT

in an arithmetical progression (1, 2, 3, 4, 5, etc. layers); then, in a
second row, in a geometric progression (1, 2, 4, 8, 16, etc. layers),
on the same paper. In both rows, contiguous steps of equal width are required.

For accurate comparison of the 2 rows -- of arithmetical and geometric increases --
precision is necessary. For this reason, water color should be avoided,
because it rarely provides even coats and always ends not only
in heavy but in unevenly heavy contours. Most advisable is the use of
film-like acetate sheets of the thinnest tints available, with adhesive backs
which provide the advantages of easy montage and invisible paste.
There are several makes, such as "Zip-a-tone," "Artype," and "Cello-tak."

In case these are not available, very thin translucent paper (waxed sandwich paper)
might demonstrate -- in transparence -- the 2 different effects,
when observed against light.

For another demonstration in turbid means -- in reflected light --
layers of thinnest whites on black paper will provide proof in an opposite direction --
the very different effects of arithmetical and geometric increase or decrease.

These studies also teach that the "decreasing increase" can be seen in the boundaries
separating the steps: In an arithmetical order of contiguous mixtures,
the boundaries gradually become softer, whereas in a geometric order the boundaries
remain equally distinct.

Such studies, of course, are only theoretically true. Because of slight material
imprecisions, the studies show occasional aberrations from the rule.

Though the Weber-Fechner Law enables "equal stepping up" (in light and in dark,
within specific hues), it is deflected by the relativity of color.

In steps which are not much wider than they are deep, these steps visually do not
remain horizontal or on an even level, as in the diagram on page 58, left.

In steps which are broader, a "fluting" effect occurs, reminiscent of the
channeling of Doric columns, as in the diagram on page 58, right.

A convincing outdoor demonstration of the Weber-Fechner Law is presented
in swimming pools painted, for example, blue. Because of reflection, the

water appears thinly tinted blue. Visually following the steps downward, one easily recognizes an increase of blueness. Since the steps are equally deep, equal amounts of blueness are added. This arithmetical physical proportion is again perceived in a decreasing geometric proporti

When the edges of the steps are compared in a downward direction they appear gradually softer. There is a double reason for this effect: First, as the increase of blueness simultaneously reduces light, the defining edges of the steps appear less clear. Second, as the increase in blueness also decreases, the contrast between neighboring blues is reduced. Consequently, the separation of the edges of the steps becomes less distinct. Both reasons follow the Weber-Fechner Law and are unrelated to any law of light refraction. Although light refraction also causes illusion in visual perception, it presents an entirely different principle because it is concerned with an optical effect. The Weber-Fechner Law explains a perceptual phenomenon.

It is surprising and unfortunate that the Weber-Fechner Law is almost unknown among colorists. Its importance is more recognized in physics -- in astronomy, electricity, and acoustics. It also proves to be important in psychology -- in the percep of sound, weight, temperature -- as well as in the perception of light and color. The presentation below of the important Weber-Fechner discovery was simplified visua and verbally for an easier understanding, but it should be emphasized that all Weber-Fechner calculations are done in logarithmic progressions which theoretically do not rea saturation points.

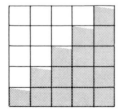 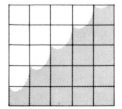

ACTUALLY PERCEIVED

XXI From color temperature to humidity in color

Earlier, when explaining light intensity as lightness and color intensity
as brightness, we found that agreement is easier in the first case,
and difficult in the second.

This is because, in defining such qualities, we deal on the one side with
physical facts and on the other with perceptual reactions
which permit either a factual measure or an interpretation of illusions.
As a result, there are in the latter case various views and opinions,
and different, if not contradictory, readings.

Any measuring of light-dark qualities is not unrelated to a scaling
of light-heavy relationships. Light-dark and light-heavy lead easily
to soft-hard comparisons; or, quick-slow and early-late connect
with young-old, and with warm-cool, as well as with wet-dry.

Such and other chain connections have led even to such opposites
as here and there, indicating spatial differentiation.

The 2 most comprehensive of the above polarities in color are first,
light-dark and light-heavy, and second, the temperature contrast
warm-cool.

In defining the placement of such contrasts within color circles,
we will see, besides their uneven distribution and their so-called
neutrals separating them, their slight overlappings of each other
when we compare one circle with the other. (See diagrams, next page.)

As to warm and cool, it is accepted in Western tradition that normally
blue appears cool and that the adjacent group, yellow-orange-red, looks warm.
As any temperature can be read higher or lower in comparison with other
temperatures, these qualifications are only relative. Therefore, there
are also warm blues and cool reds possible within their own hues.

But when these temperature indicators, red and blue, are combined with color neutrals, as whites, blacks, and greys, and with their mixtures, particularly in mixtures with the temperature neutrals green and violet, then personal interpretations of temperatures may easily become disparate.

Therefore, it will be comprehensible that such theories of interpretation may lead to and end in personal beliefs. So it is not surprising that the warm-cool principle in color which successfully dominated the Munich school of painting around the turn of the century resulted finally in fruitless controversies.

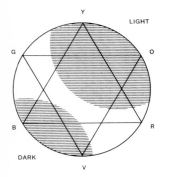 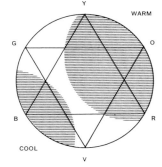 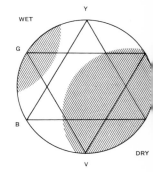

It was successful in gaining followers by offering a theory for defining spatial relationship of colors, through their higher and lower illusional temperature. As this warm-cool relationship was closely connected with the light-dark contrast, the hardest but apparently lasting conversion then was that light was cold and shadows warm, at least outdoors. It split up in factions of different beliefs about the function of cool and warm with regard to spatial directions in painting, whether the <u>here</u> contra <u>there</u> was decisive, or the <u>above</u> contra <u>below</u>, or the <u>in</u> contra <u>out</u>. A clear example of these opposites is the contrast between Boucher's receding deepening with vermilion red, and Rubens' advancing heightening with white.

All this may be a reason why the warm-cool contrast is not in fashion today, although a new theory declares warm near and cool far, because the former is of longer and the latter of shorter wave length, and they are, therefore, optically registered in different ways. But optical and perceptual registration are not necessarily parallel.

XXII Vibrating boundaries -- enforced contours

As a deception, this effect is related to our earlier experience
in which 2 colors appeared as 3 or 4 colors.

However, the additional illusionary colors
often are hard to define as to their hue.

They often appear as shadow on one side of the boundary
and as light reflected on the other side.

Or sometimes this vibration presents just a duplication
or triplication of the boundary line.

The conditions for these varying effects occur between colors
which are contrasting in their hues but also close or similar
in light intensity.

Though this effect refers to the after-image,
its physio-psychological function apparently
seems not to have been clarified.

Often, under the same conditions, it is perceived by some people
and not by others.

It is visible and not visible with or without glasses;
or, similarly, with interchanging of near and far focus.

This initially exciting effect also feels aggressive
and often even uncomfortable to our eyes.
One finds it rarely used except for a screaming effect
in advertising, and as a result it is unpleasant, disliked, and avoided.

Equal light intensity -- vanishing boundaries

Though rarely perceived, it is a fact that articulate boundaries
between colors can be made nearly unrecognizable, or made practically
invisible -- through the choice of color alone.

This very surprising and most exciting of all color phenomena depends,
like all other effects, on specific conditions.

The effect is the opposite of the aforementioned vibrating boundaries,
and it is not possible between very contrasting hues.
It is confined to adjacent, neighboring colors and depends most decisively
on equal "light intensity." Only real equality in lightness
or an equivalent real equality in darkness produces the effect here aimed at
and searched for.

Now, since the term "equal value" has unfortunately been misused too often
for colors lacking just this quality, incompetent judgment has distorted
this term to a falsified measure. In this way, "equal values"
are more spoken about than realized -- than actually seen.

Thus, we can safely state that very few people -- including many colorists
and painters -- have ever seen 2 adjacent colors
of true equal light value -- that is, of exact equality in light,
of the same level of light, or, in a sense, the same altitude of light.

This will indicate that equal light intensity presents,
besides a most challenging exercise, a most difficult task
demanding most of all -- patience.

Because several of our color classes were not able to present
even 1 convincing color couple of equal light intensity,
this makes it an exercise for teachers willing to demonstrate
that in all teaching the personal example is the strongest incentive.

Earlier, right after the test "Which is the lighter and/or darker?"
we had the opportunity to prepare for this difficult exercise,
which usually is the last exercise of our course.

When we were collecting pairs of colors hard to distinguish as lighter or darker
we were often tempted to
consider some of them to be of "equal value."

At that time we learned that in cases difficult to decide upon,
which we named "near-equal light intensities," or "almost-equals,"
the after-image test can be a helpful measure. (See diagram, page 13.)

Though sometimes it may appear hopeless to find equal light intensities in paint
and painting, in color papers, or in our surroundings, we have found that
nature occasionally provides an opportunity to see them on cumulus clouds
against blue sky.

When these clouds, often lined up in horizontal groups,
appear gleaming white in their upper part in full sunlight,
separated from and rising against a distant deep blue,
then underneath they show grey tones as shaded white.
These shades merge, or even hinge, with the same
but here very close blue. Why very close? This grey is
of the same light intensity as the neighboring blue below.
Thus, the boundaries between grey and blue vanish,
and we do not see where clouds end and where sky begins.
With such clouds, this is best observed with the sun at our backs.

(See Plate XXIII -- 2.)

In order to produce this provocative color effect -- but also the most
delicate one -- all disturbing effects of paper (such as different surfaces)
and of montage (visible edges or paste marks) must be carefully avoided.

Therefore, the 2 papers of equal light intensity must be mounted as inlay (known also as "intarsia").

In this process the papers are placed within each other, instead of on top of each other. Thus the thickness of the paper does not show, and, more important, its very disturbing shadows are eliminated -- provided the papers are of equal thickness.

For precision fitting, so that the joints will not show, the papers to be inlaid are formed simultaneously in a single cutting.

The finer the knife (best, the thinnest razor blade), the thinner the paper, and the harder the ground to cut on (preferably glass), the better the fitting will be and the less the joints will show. It is also essential that no glue seep in to mark the joints.

As the selection of the papers here demands patience, so their presentation demands skill and cleanliness.

XXIV Color theories -- color systems

Originally, we began our color course with a presentation
of various color systems, of color theories.

With the discovery that color is the most relative medium in art, and that
its greatest excitement lies beyond rules and canons,
a more sensitive discrimination was needed.

The more a creative use of color developed, the less desirable became
a merely trustful and obedient application.

The seeing of color became our first concern.

As a result, we came to present color systems not at the beginning
but at the end of our course.

We learned that their beautiful order is more recognized and appreciated
when eyes and mind are -- after productive exercises --
better prepared and more receptive.
In a laboratory course as described, it is not the ambition
to provide a comprehensive knowledge of many theories.
We can introduce only briefly the most important systems, which are
systematic groupings of the colors of the visible sun spectrum,
presented in 2-dimensional or 3-dimensional order.
However, we encourage extended interest in private study of theories.

In presenting systems showing organized color relationship,
we usually start with the rarely published, beautiful Goethe Triangle. (See back cove

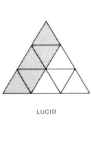

LUCID

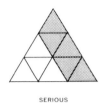

SERIOUS

MIGHTY

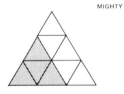

SERENE

MELANCHOLIC

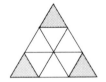

PRIMARIES

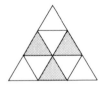

SECONDARIES

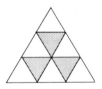

TERTIARIES

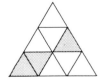

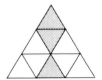

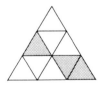

COMPLEMENTARIES WITH THEIR MIXTURES WHICH ARE DOMINATED BY THEIR PRIMARIES

We then refer to Schopenhauer's experiment on the relation and balance
of light with quantity within the color wheel, as explained on page 43.

Of the contemporary systems, we present and analyze briefly the order
of the Munsell Color Tree, as well as the Ostwald Color System,
and show an offspring of the latter, the Faber Birren Color System.

Besides the difference in measurements within these systems,
we point out their practical value for industrial uses.

We also show the limitations of the systems,
particularly in connection with painting.
Only the Munsell System presents a calculation of color quantity
with regard to area extension, without counting an additional
effect through recurrence.

We emphasize that color harmonies, usually the special interest
or aim of color systems, are not the only desirable relationship.
As with tones in music, so with color -- dissonance is as desirable
as its opposite, consonance.
After such brief introduction to established color systems
we introduce a more recent, most important development,
the spectrophotometer, for automatic color analysis.

Since no purpose is served by going into further details of color systems,
it seems worth while to distinguish 3 basically different approaches
to color based upon the different interests of
the physicist, the psychologist, and the colorist.
To indicate only a single difference: whereas the primary colors
for the colorist (painters, designers) are, as we know, yellow-red-blue,
the physicist has 3 other primaries (not including yellow),
and the psychologist counts 4 primaries (the fourth being green),
plus 2 neutrals, white and black.

XXV   On teaching color -- some color terms

In the previous chapters we have presented a studio course,
or, if you prefer, a laboratory or workshop course
which opposes an administrative attitude of "theory and practice."
Naturally, practice is not preceded but followed by theory.
Such study promotes a more lasting teaching and learning
through experience. Its aim is development of creativeness
realized in discovery and invention -- the criteria of creativity,
or flexibility, being imagination and fantasy. Altogether
it promotes "thinking in situations," a new educational concept
unfortunately little known and less cultivated, so far.

We have described, up to now, the basic color problems to be solved,
and have presented them in a logical sequence in which each problem
prepares for following ones.

The color plates selected for reproduction in this edition are strictly studies,
that is, experimental tryouts. They aim at 1 distinct effect only, which,
at the time, was given as an exercise, obligatory for all members of the class.
These exercises are not meant to illustrate, or to decorate or beautify
something, but aim at the development of the ability to produce the
desired color effects. This reiterates our disbelief in self-expression, either
as a way of study or as its aim, in schools.

After too much non-teaching, non-learning, and a consequent non-seeing,
-- in too many art "activities" -- it is time to advocate again a basic
step-by-step learning which promotes recognition of insight coming
from experience, and evaluation resulting from comparison.
This, in sum, means recognition of development and improvement,
that is, of growth, growth of ability. This growth is not only
a most exciting experience; it is inspiring and thus
the strongest incentive for intensified action, for continued investigation
(search instead of re-search), for learning through conscious practice.

Gestalt psychology has proved that 3-dimensionality is perceived earlier
and more easily than 2-dimensionality. This explains why
children do not begin -- as most art teachers still wish -- with
painting and drawing, which are lateral abstractions on a
2-dimensional plane, but begin all by themselves with building,
constructing in space, on a ground and upward, in 3 dimensions.

We believe that art education is an essential part of
general education, including so-called higher learning.
We promote, therefore, after a natural and easy laissez-faire
as an initial challenge, an early shift from aimless play to
directed study and work, which offers, with a basic training,
a continuous excitement of growth.

To say this in psychological-educational terms, it means
a shift from a recognition of the first but primitive drive
for being occupied, entertained -- Beschäftigungstrieb --
to a more advanced drive, or better, need, for being
productive, creative -- Gestaltungstrieb.

The results of our trial-and-error experimentation, mostly done after
class, are exhibited at the beginning of the next class. (These studies
we call the "admission tickets" to the class.)

They are then compared and evaluated by the entire class, students and
teacher. First, every class member makes his selection and
compares his preferences with his own contributions. Then, we
-- that is, the teacher or a student or students -- select the best examples
of "psychological engineering." This qualification we confer on a
convincing presentation because it eliminates misleading reading of the
study's purpose and its desired effect.

The normal procedure in presenting a new problem often is to show a sample
exercise and to point to its specific effect. The class is then asked to
produce equal effects with similar and other colors -- without first being
told how to do it.

After a while, a collection of the first trials -- wrong as well as
"on the way" or right -- will give an opportunity to lead, to direct,
to point at (or to indicate only by comparison forth and back) new
ways of promising investigation.

It comes as a pleasant surprise in a step-by-step learning that the further
the course proceeds, the more each succeeding problem is accidentally
if not actually presented among the studies shown at the beginning of a
class. The teacher may prefer to present the new problem with this
"step ahead" (thus evading his own prepared presentation), as a new
direction emanating from the class. This "step ahead" will prove a most
contagious stimulus to the class.

As basic rules of any language must be practiced continuously, and
therefore are never fixed, so exercises toward distinct color effects
never are done or over. New and different cases will be discovered
time and again, and should be presented to the class again and again. In
this way the study will be a mutual give and take. It will also show that
all thorough study is basic, and that all education is self-education.
This indicates that we expect from every student several solutions
to each problem.

In the end, teaching is a matter not of method but of heart. Therefore,
the most decisive factor is the teacher's personality. His enthusiastic
concern with the student's growth counts more than how much he knows. It
is well known that "the teacher is always right," but rarely does this fact
elicit respect or sympathy; even less often does it prove competence
and authority.

But the teacher actually is right and always will gain confidence
when he admits that he does not know, that he cannot decide, and,
as it often is with color, that he is unable to make a choice
or to give advice.

Besides, good teaching is more a giving of right questions
than a giving of right answers.

A few color terms which need additional explanation

Relativity:
The length of any object is relative to the length
of longer or shorter objects. Thus, any in-between length, seen in 2 different
relationships, presents 2 different values. Therefore, changing measure
results in changing evaluations.

In a similar way, as we learned before, 1 temperature can feel as 2.
Also, weight may be registered in different ways. If, of 3 hands,
the first holds only a small sheet of paper, the second a pile of
sheets or a book, and the third a pile of books, then physically
each of the 3 hands is exposed to weight. The first will feel nothing
or only a soft touch, the second clearly some pressure downward, and
the third may even feel pain.

Relativity is caused by a variance of measure, by lack or avoidance of
standard rules, or by changing viewpoints. As a result, 1 phenomenon
has varying views, readings, and different meanings.

This instability of value is extremely characteristic of color. Resulting
from the after-image, a light grey, for instance, may look dark at one
time and almost white at another, and at various times like a shade or a tint
of any color, as green may look reddish.

The purpose of most of our color studies is to prove that color is
the most relative medium in art, that we almost never perceive
what color is physically.

The mutual influencing of colors we call -- interaction.
Seen from the opposite viewpoint, it is -- interdependence.

Though we were taught, only a few years ago, that there is no connection
whatever between visual and auditory perception, we know now that a color
changes visually when a changing tone is heard simultaneously. This,
of course, makes the relativity of color still more obvious, just as
tongue and eye perceptions interdepend when colors of food and of its
containers increase or diminish our appetite.

Factual -- Actual:
In dealing with color relativity or color illusion, it is practical
to distinguish factual facts from actual facts.

The data on wave length -- the result of optical analysis of light spectra --
we acknowledge as fact.

This is a factual fact.

It means something remaining what it is, something probably not undergoing changes.

But when we see opaque color as transparent or perceive opacity as translucence, then the optical reception in our eye has changed in our mind to something different. The same is true when we see 3 colors as 4 or as 2, or 4 colors as 3, when we see flat, even colors as intersecting colors and their fluting effect, or when we see distinct 1-contour boundaries doubled or vibrating or just vanishing.

These effects we call actual facts.

This kind of fact seems parallel to the common saying, "what actually happened," that is, what happened in time, what went on, what moved, what developed.

But "actual size" usually means something fixed, something remaining permanent, standing still. Therefore, "factual size" would be more truthful because "actual" is related to "action." It is something not fixed, but changing with time.

"Action" is the noun for the verb "to act." Acting in visual presentation is to change by giving up, by losing identity. When we act, we change appearance and behavior, we act as someone else.

For further clarification, therefore, actors who present only themselves remain always the same. They may appear interesting, but they do not act. In our terms they remain factual. However, when an actor is able to appear as Henry VIII, so that we overlook or forget who he factually is, and when he also can be expected to play Henry IX or Henry X, then he is a real actor, able to give up his own identity and present someone else's appearance and personality.

Color acts in a similar way. Because of the after-image (the simultaneous contrast), colors influence and change each other forth and back. They continuously interact -- in our perception.

Value:
The word as such, when unspecified, permits application in innumerable directions. By itself, it does not reveal on what level, in what direction or field evaluation is meant.

73

In color, it is a distinct measure only in connection with the Munsell System. There, Munsell defines value as the lightness of a color. In connection with other systems it has no outspoken meaning. The French word <u>valeur</u> has a broader meaning. Unfortunately, the careless use of "value," particularly with regard to equal lightness -- as well as false examples reproduced in books -- has destroyed it as a means of measure. Therefore we use "light intensity" instead as a self-explanatory term. (See Chapters V, page 12, and XXIII, page 63.)

Variants versus variety

The word variety, although recently a favored design term,
has become discredited because of increased abuse. It has
become a pretentious recommendation for designs of questionable merit.
It is applied to protect hurried changes, to excuse poor alterations,
or to defend any accidental and meaningless whim. It even appears
as a weapon to prevent rejection, to force credits. Thus the excuse
"for variety's sake" remains a warning signal.

To replace this negative criterion, we are in favor of a related word
of better reputation, the design term "variant." As variety usually
concerns changes of details, variant means a more thorough re-doing of
a whole or of a part within a given scheme. Although variant may remind us
slightly of imitative plagiarism, normally it results from a
thorough study. Because of a more comprehensive comparison
forth and back, it usually aims at a new presentation. On the whole,
variants demonstrate, besides a sincere attitude, a healthy belief
that there is no final solution in form; thus form demands unending
performance and invites constant reconsideration -- visually as well as verbally.

This book presents results of search, not of what is academically called
research.
As it is not a compilation from books, it does not end with a list of
books -- either books read, or books not read.
Instead, this book ends with an acknowledgment of my students who are the
authors of the sample studies, and whom I therefore consider my indirect but
first collaborators.

In addition to the dedication of this book, I should like to state
that my students in color have taught me more color than have books
about color.

Many students of this color course (which has been developed in the United States)
not only have found solutions of their own to known problems, but also
have visualized and discovered new problems, new solutions, and new
presentations. Although rarely shown, and therefore barely known so far,
their contributions deserve publication in the interest of a new
intensified training of eyes and minds -- in both art education and
general education.

Those contributions come from 2 sides, from a majority of normally
gifted students, as well as from the minority of more gifted students.
And particularly this majority has taught me how to proceed, how to
open eyes and minds; even more important, it has taught me
what not to do.

We should have liked to name here the authors of all the sample studies
reproduced in the first edition. Unfortunately, many names are lacking,
uncertain, or lost. The known names are listed alphabetically in the original
edition, followed by the numbers of the folders containing their studies.